My Little BRAVERY BLANKET

PETER PAUPER PRESS, INC.
Rye Brook, New York

PETER PAUPER PRESS

In 1928, at the age of twenty-two, Peter Beilenson began printing books on a small press in the basement of his parents' home in Larchmont, New York. Peter—and later, his wife, Edna—sought to create fine books that sold at "prices even a pauper could afford."

Today, still family owned and operated, Peter Pauper Press continues to honor our founders' legacy of quality, value, and fun for big kids and small kids alike.

Written by Hannah Beilenson
Designed by Heather Zschock

3 International Drive
Rye Brook, NY 10573 USA

Published in the UK and Europe by Peter Pauper Press, Inc.
c/o White Pebble International
Units 2-3, Spring Business Park
Stanbridge Road
Havant, Hampshire PO9 2GJ, UK

ISBN 978-1-4413-4209-6
Printed in China

7 6 5 4 3 2 1

Visit us at www.peterpauper.com

OUR ACTIONS AND US

Have you ever tried something new? Shared a toy or snack? Given a hug or high five when someone needed it? Well, those are just a few examples of putting your feelings into action! And every action you take can make a change. You can make people smile and laugh, help others feel safe, and create something new for everyone to share. There's so much you can do, and there's no wrong place to start—so let's take action today!

One action is **Bravery**, and we'll meet someone who will help us learn more about it.

The thunder is so loud! I don't know what to do.
Yeah, it's pretty scary.

Who are you?
I'm a **Bravery Blanket**. I help you show courage.
But I already know what it means to be brave.

Brave people are
heroes.

They do scary things,
and they help people.

And they're not afraid of anything.
But that's not true!
It isn't?

I'm so high up!
People can be brave and scared at the same time.

I'm so far
from home.
If things weren't scary,
there'd be no reason
to be brave.

But how can I feel scared and brave at the same time?
Because bravery isn't something you feel, it's something you do.

When you're
nervous or afraid,
but you choose
to try something
new,

or stand up for what you believe in,

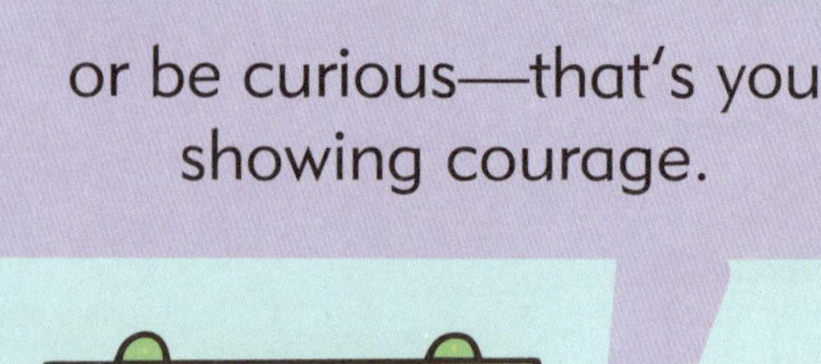
or be curious—that's you
showing courage.

That makes sense.
But it sounds kind of hard.

Sometimes it is hard. But showing courage can lead to great things.
Really?

Yes! When you're brave, you
can have fun,

you can help other people,

and you can learn something, too! Then the things you were afraid of start to shrink.
Yeah. Now that I know more about thunder, it doesn't seem so loud anymore.

But thunder is a small thing to be brave against.

Some acts of bravery are small, but that doesn't mean they're unimportant.

Every time you choose to be brave, you make it easier for others to be brave, too.

And every time you show courage for something small, it becomes easier to show courage for larger things.
I think I get it. When I show bravery, I gain bravery, too.

And now that the storm has passed, there's so much to do!

Meet My Bravery Blanket

My Bravery Blanket's name is:

....

I feel scared when:

....

....

....

I can be brave by:

....

....

....

....